Learning By Drawing

Amazing Animals

Basic Word Types

Colin M. Drysdale

Illustrated by _____

Pictish Beast Publications

Text Copyright © 2017 Colin M. Drysdale
Imprint and Layout Copyright © 2017 Colin M. Drysdale/Pictish Beast Publications

All rights reserved.
No part of this book shall be reproduced, stored in a retrieval system, or transmitted by any means, electronic, mechanical, photocopying, recording, or otherwise without permission from the author.

If you wish to use any of the contents of this book for educational purposes, including photocopying individual pages to create handouts for use in classrooms, an educational licence, which allows you to legally do this, can be purchased from *www.pictishbeastpublications.com/learning-by-drawing*.

ISBN - 978-1-909832-36-7

Published by Pictish Beast Publications, Glasgow, UK.
Published in the United Kingdom
First Printing: 2017. First Edition.

This is a work of fiction.
Any resemblance to anyone, or any animals, living or, dead is purely coincidental.

The cover image is copyright of C.M. Drysdale

www.PictishBeastPublications.com

Boring Stuff For Grown-ups To Read
How To Use This Book

This book is designed for children, aged six and older, to introduce them to the concept of basic word types by drawing animals from short, funny descriptions. Through these drawings, they learn about nouns, pronouns, adjectives, verbs and adverbs, and how they work together to make sentences and bring writing to life.

For children at the youngest end of this age range, read the description of the animal with them, and then ask them to draw it. Older children can read the description themselves before drawing the animal. Once they have finished their drawing, you can then show the child how each word type in the description relates to a specific aspect of their drawing: Nouns are represented as discrete objects on the page (i.e. anything that has an outline in their picture); pronouns help provide additional information about what these nouns are like without having to repeat the nouns themselves; adjectives are the characteristics of these objects (such as their colour or shape); verbs are what they are doing (such as walking or running); and adverbs are how they are doing it (e.g. quickly or slowly).

No matter what age of child you are giving this book to, remember there is no right or wrong drawing to go with each animal (and if you have more than one child make sure that the older one does not tell the younger one that their drawing is wrong!). The idea is that children are given the freedom to imagine each animal from the description given and then draw a picture of it. In addition to learning about basic word types, this will help them develop their interpretation of words, their drawing and coordination skills, and their imaginations!

If you are an educator and you wish to use any of the contents of this book for educational purposes, an educational licence (which allows you to legally photocopy pages to create handouts) can be purchased from *www.pictishbeastpublications.com/learning-by-drawing*. Ideas for classroom activities to accompany this book can also be accessed through this webpage.

"Hi there!

"I like **animals**, and I have **many weird** and **Wonderful** pets.

"If I **tell** you what they **look** like, will you **draw** pictures of them for **me**?"

Dr Colin - The Cryptozoologist

Nouns

Nouns are words that represent discrete objects (or concepts). They are the things that a sentence is about. In your drawings of the *Amazing Animals* featured in this book, they will be anything with an outline, such as the animal itself, individual parts of its body, the clothes it is wearing and the things it is holding. For the descriptions of the first two animals in this section, each noun is <u>underlined</u> to help you spot them. See if you can spot, and underline, the nouns on your own in the third description.

Hammy

Hammy is a hamster. He has green fur, and he likes to wear a bright red hat.

Draw what you think Hammy the hamster looks like here:

Jeffrey

Jeffrey is a **giraffe**. He has a l o n g neck, and he **likes** to wear a very l o n g **pink** scarf that is covered in **yellow** and **red** stripes.

Draw what you think Jeffrey the giraffe looks like here:

See if you can <u>underline</u> all the nouns in this description of Charlie the chimpanzee.

Charlie

Charlie is a **chimpanzee**. He likes to wear **roller skates** on his **feet** and he plays the **guitar** as he skates around my **house**. He also likes to wear a **pink** tutu!

Draw what you think Charlie the chimpanzee looks like here:

Pronouns

Pronouns are short words, such as he, she, it, them, his and hers, that are used in place of a noun. A pronoun is directly linked to the specific noun it replaces and which is used elsewhere in a sentence (or in a previous sentence in the same paragraph). In the descriptions of the *Amazing Animals* featured in this book, pronouns are used to provide more information about a specific noun that forms part of your drawing. For the descriptions of the first two animals in this section, each pronoun is <u>underlined</u> to help you spot them. See if you can spot, and underline, the pronouns on your own in the third description. Similarly, as you read through the descriptions, draw an arrow linking each pronoun to its associated noun to help you identify it.

Sammy

Sammy is a **seal**. <u>She</u> has **blue** skin, and **yellow** spots. <u>She</u> wears **orange** armbands to help **her** swim.

Draw what you think Sammy the seal looks like here:

Armando

Armando is an armadillo. He wears red shoes and pink fairy wings. He also wears a spotty bow tie and a black top hat.

Draw what you think Armando the armadillo looks like here:

See if you can <u>underline</u> all the pronouns in this description of Dino the diplodocus.

Dino

Dino is a Diplodocus. He has a very **long** neck and a very **long** tail. He uses his **long** neck to reach over **fences** and walls, and he **likes** to eat all the **RED** flowers from my **neighbour's** garden.

Draw what you think Dino the diplodocus looks like here:

Adjectives

Adjectives are words that tell you more about the objects represented by the nouns or pronouns in a sentence. This means that each adjective is linked to a specific noun, or pronoun, and you cannot use adjectives on their own. In your drawings of the *Amazing Animals* featured in this book, the adjectives will be things like the colours you use to draw an animal, its shape and size, and the patterns on its clothes. For the descriptions of the first two animals in this section, each adjective is <u>underlined</u> to help you spot them. See if you can spot, and underline, the adjectives on your own in the third description. Similarly, as you read through the descriptions, draw an arrow linking each adjective to its associated noun or pronoun to help you identify it.

Ginny

Ginny is a guinea pig. She likes to wear a **yellow** dress with **green** spots on it, and she likes to **dance** around my **house** like a **ballerina**.

Draw what you think Ginny the guinea pig looks like here:

Garry

Garry is a **gorilla**. He is <u>very</u> **big** and **strong**, and he can lift my **motorbike** over his **head** with one **hand**. He has a <u>long</u> **green** moustache, a <u>tiny</u> **purple** beard, and **bright blue** eyebrows.

Draw what you think Garry the gorilla looks like here:

See if you can <u>underline</u> all the adjectives in this description of Danny the dog.

Danny

Danny is a **dog**. He is a **dachshund**. This means he has a very **long** body and very **short** legs, but unlike most dachshunds, he is **bright green**, with **yellow** and **pink** stripes. His favourite toy is a very **large** black ball that he likes to chase, but his very **short** legs make it difficult to run **fast** enough to catch it.

Draw what you think Danny the dog looks like here:

Verbs

Verbs are doing words. They tell you more about what a noun, or pronoun, in a sentence is doing. This includes 'being', so words like *am*, *is* and *has* are also verbs. Like an adjective, each verb is linked to a specific noun or pronoun, and you cannot use verbs on their own. In your drawings of the *Amazing Animals* featured in this book, the verbs will be what the animals are doing, such as running, walking or playing. For the descriptions of the first two animals in this section, each verb is underlined to help you spot them. See if you can spot, and underline, the verbs on your own in the third description. Similarly, as you read through the descriptions, draw an arrow linking each verb to its associated noun, or pronoun, to help you identify it.

Mike

Mike is a monkey. He is covered in red and blue stripes and he sings funny songs as he swings from tree to tree.

Draw what you think Mike the monkey looks like here:

Polly

Polly **is** a **parrot**. She **has** **green** wings and an **orange** head, and she **speaks** **five** different languages. She **dresses** like a **clown** so she **can** **make** all the other animals **laugh**.

Draw what you think Polly the parrot looks like here:

See if you can <u>underline</u> all the verbs in this description of Samantha the snake.

Samantha

Samantha is a **snake**. She is very, very **long**, and she likes to curl up in front of the fire in my living room. Her head is **blue**, her body is **green** and her tail is **yellow** with **red** spots. This means that people often **mistake** her for a brightly coloured **scarf**, and when they try to put her on, they get a very **big shock**!

Draw what you think Samantha the snake looks like here:

Adverbs

Adverbs are words that tell you how things are being done. This means that each adverb is linked to a specific verb in a sentence, and you cannot use adverbs on their own. In your drawings of the *Amazing Animals* featured in this book, the adverbs will tell you how the animals are doing the things they are doing, such as running fast. For the descriptions of the first two animals in this section, each adverb is <u>underlined</u> to help you spot them. See if you can spot, and underline, the adverbs on your own in the third description. Similarly, As you read through the descriptions, draw an arrow linking each adverb to its associated verb to help you identify it.

Matt

Matt is a **bat**. He has **pink** wings, and **big** blue ears, and he **likes** to fly <u>fast</u> through the **forest** where he lives. He likes ice cream made from **insects** and he eats it <u>very noisily</u>. He lives in the **tropics** where it is **very** warm, so whenever he gets **ice cream** he has to eat it <u>**quickly**</u> before it melts all over his face.

Draw what you think Matt the bat looks like here:

Kenny

Kenny is a kangaroo. Kenny has big green eyes and blue fur. He is a very happy kangaroo and he really likes to bounce around. Sometimes he bounces quickly, and sometimes he bounces slowly, and one time he bounced right over the top of my house!

Draw what you think Kenny the kangaroo looks like here:

See if you can <u>underline</u> all the adverbs in this description of Eddie the eagle.

Eddie

Eddie is an **eagle**. He has a **white** head and a long sharp, **yellow** beak. He is from a place called **America** and he really likes to dress like a **cowboy**. He wears a **large blue** hat, a **green** jacket and **orange** trousers. While most eagles like to fly high in the air, soaring slowly above the clouds, **Eddie** is very scared of heights. This means he has to walk **everywhere** he wants to go!

Draw what you think Eddie the eagle looks like here:

Bringing It All Together

In this section, you will find descriptions of two new animals. However, none of the words in these descriptions have been underlined. Once you have drawn each animal, go back to the description and underline the nouns in red, the pronouns in orange, the adjectives in blue, the verbs in green and the adverbs in yellow, and then draw coloured arrows to link the pronouns to their associated nouns; adjectives and verbs to their associated nouns or pronouns; and adverbs to their associated verbs. If you need help doing this, you can look back at your drawing, remembering that the nouns are anything with an outline; the pronouns replace nouns used elsewhere to provide more information without having to repeat them; the adjectives describe what the nouns, or pronouns, look like; the verbs are what the nouns are doing; and the adverbs are how they are doing it. For the final animal in this book, you will need to write your own description, using your knowledge of what nouns, pronouns adjectives, verbs and adverbs are, before drawing a picture of it.

Ellie

Ellie is an **elephant**. She is very **big**, and she has a **long** trunk and very **large** ears. Her skin is **grey**, but she likes to wear a **red** jumper with **large** white spots on it. She likes to dance wildly and **everywhere** she goes she listens to music on her **headphones**.

Draw what you think Ellie the elephant looks like here:

Deborah

Deborah is a zebra. Most normal zebras have **black** and white stripes, but Deborah is not a **normal** zebra. Her stripes are **red**, and **orange** and **yellow** and **green** and blue and **violet**. This makes her look just like a rainbow! She loves to play **hide-and-seek**, but because she is so brightly coloured, it is **always** very easy for the other **animals** to find her.

Draw what you think Deborah the zebra looks like here:

Simon

This time it is your turn to come up with an animal I might like to have as a pet! Think of what type of animal Simon is, what he looks like, what he wears and what he likes to do, and then draw a picture of him on the page opposite. Once you have finished your drawing, write a description for him, making sure you underline all the nouns, pronouns, adjectives, verbs and adverbs in different colours, and use arrows to link them together in the correct way.

Draw what you imagine Simon looks like here:

Dedication

This book is dedicated to all who like to read and draw, regardless of their age!

www.ingramcontent.com/pod-product-compliance
Lightning Source LLC
Chambersburg PA
CBHW081127080526
44587CB00021B/3784